How The New Marriage Law
Helped Chinese Women Stand Up

Edited and translated by
Susan Glosser

Published by Opal Mogus Books
2005

The original was edited by Dong Jianzhi,
illustrated by Cheng Shifa and published by
New Tide Publishing Company, Shanghai,
November, 1950.

Susan Glosser teaches Chinese history at Lewis and Clark College in Portland, Oregon. Her first book, *Chinese Visions of Family and State, 1915-1953* (Berkeley: University of California Press, 2003), traces the development of the conjugal family ideal in China and explores the ways in which various political and reformist groups used this ideal to speak about their visions of a strong Chinese state.

Library of Congress Control Number: 2005931585

*For my students
at Lewis & Clark College*

Table of Contents

Editor's Prologue

 I found this pamphlet in a small pile of books on a sidewalk in Shanghai in 1993 at the informal antique bazaar that appeared every Saturday morning not far from the famous Li family garden. As it happened, I was in Shanghai researching family reform in the Republican era (1911-1949) and the early PRC (People's Republic of China).

This pamphlet was published six months after the promulgation of the New Marriage Law in April 1950 and was part of the PRC's early efforts to educate the populace about marriage and divorce laws. It appears to have belonged to the library of a Shanghai cotton mill. Individuals may have borrowed these pamphlets to read on their own. It is also likely that such pamphlets were used in adult education classes.

Li Fengjin's comic-book format was intended to appeal to people of limited literacy—the vocabulary is small, the prose direct, and much of the story can be gleaned from the illustrations alone. The editor of the pamphlet, Dong Jianzhi, assumed that the audience knew much more about traditional practices and prejudices than it did about the New Marriage Law. The narrative sentences that accompany many of the frames tell the reader exactly how to understand the characters' actions. Throughout the pamphlet, the principles behind the PRC's marriage and divorce laws and its key articles on marriage and divorce rights are introduced in a manner that leaves no room for misinterpretation. The exceptions to this rule are found in the two frames on page eight. In the top frame, the heroine leans on the doorframe in a manner that would traditionally have been considered provocative. (As my student Antonia Mays pointed out, think of the depraved Pan Jinlian in the first chapters of *Plum in the Golden Vase*, who attracted the attention of male passersby as she loitered in her doorway.) In the second, Gu and Li sit side by side at the end of a secluded lane, behavior that would be considered improper for a married couple and entirely scandalous for an unmarried one. My hunch is that the creators of the pamphlet included these images so that their traditional-minded readers could be confronted with situations they found improper and then taught that, in fact, such interactions between unmarried men and women were acceptable.

It occurred to me that the effort that went into making the text an effective educational tool for China's workers and farmers also made it an ideal source for the classroom. To that end I have translated the pamphlet in its entirety, but otherwise left it in its original form. In order to provide historical context, I have written a brief introduction and provided notes for individual frames. The appendix reproduces the PRC's New Marriage Law of 1950. A selected bibliography lists the many secondary sources that I have drawn on in my research.

A number of people have improved this project with their observations and suggestions. First and foremost I would like to thank the students who participated in my seminar on the history of Chinese family and gender in the spring of 2002 and the spring of 2004—Kristen Aaker, Andrea Biehn, Patrick Cronin, Holly Fern, Joleen Fuller, Jered Gorman, Janida Grima, Rebecca Hayes, Kirtlye Lohof, Antonia Mays, Patrick Newsham, Niji Riegler, Amber Schaub, Cecelia Shroyer, and Elizabeth Walleri. Many thanks to Lyell Asher, Carlton Benson, Patty Stranahan, Edward Rhoads, and Jeff Wasserstrom for their valuable comments and corrections. I am indebted to Stephen Dow Beckham for his encouragement and advice on how to establish a small press. Jovanna Schussel did much of the scanning and typing for the pamphlet and wrestled the English translations into the small dialogue boxes meant for the much more succinct Chinese. I am grateful to Jeanne Galick for her expertise and creativity in the design and layout of the cover and English sections. I would also like to thank Lewis & Clark College for the subvention grant that made this publication possible.

With the exception of the English translation and some reformatting of the cover, the pamphlet appears here as it did originally. Please note that within the frames the narrative is meant to be read first, and it usually works best to read the dialogue boxes from left to right.

I have done my best to obtain permission to republish this pamphlet and to reprint the codes in the appendices, but to date have been unsuccessful. I would appreciate hearing from anyone who has contact information for permissions requests or biographical information on the editor or illustrator.

Introduction

In April 1950 as one of its first pieces of legislation, the government of the People's Republic of China passed the New Marriage Law. The highlights of the law were the articles that guaranteed the individual's right to marry whomever he or she chose and the right to divorce. The promulgation of the New Marriage Law was accompanied by great fanfare and even greater claims. The Chinese Communist Party (CCP) portrayed itself as the solitary champion of women's rights. It also asserted, as the title of the law suggested, that its legislation was an unprecedented breakthrough for women's rights and the first significant effort to dismantle the "feudal" family system.

In the historiography of China, the first of these claims has been reevaluated. A number of scholars have examined the CCP's diligence in promoting women's rights and marriage reform. Their efforts have revealed that from the early years of the Jiangxi Soviet, the Party backed away from its efforts to institute gender equality and marriage reform whenever such efforts threatened to cost the Party the support of the rural population. Even at the moment that the New Marriage Law was put into effect, the government advised local cadres to give priority to land reform over marriage reform. It appears that although the CCP advanced women's rights and family reform, it did so cautiously and in a limited fashion. However, the second of the CCP's claims, that its marriage law was unprecedented in China's history, has not been as closely examined. In fact, the 1950 law was preceded by over three decades of philosophical debate, civil legislation, and social practice.

Arguably the earliest antecedent of family reform was Chinese intellectuals' interest in the principles of Social Darwinism. Social Darwinism was introduced to the Chinese intelligentsia at the end of the nineteenth-century by Yan Fu (1854-1921) through his translations of the writings of Thomas Huxley (1825-1895) and Herbert Spencer (1820-1903). The first of these translations followed hard on China's humiliating defeat by the Japanese in the Sino-Japanese war of 1895. The idea that societies, like organisms, needed to evolve in order to survive excited many of China's intellectuals.

China had fully expected its newly modernized navy to defeat the Japanese in 1895, but it took the Japanese only about four hours to put half of the Chinese fleet on the bottom of the sea. The principles of Social Darwinism provided both an explanation for China's failure to repulse the encroachments of foreign powers and a program for change. Clearly the *tiyong* formula suggested by the accomplished general and civil official Zhang Zhidong (1837-1909) in the late 1890s —maintain Chinese essence but use Western technology—was insufficient to ensure China's survival. Many intellectuals concluded that Chinese culture was obsolete: China's survival depended not only on the adoption of Western technology, but also on a radical evolution of Chinese culture and a remaking of its very essence.

This radical reevaluation of Chinese culture peaked with the New Culture Movement (1915-1923). During this period, Chinese students and intellectuals questioned practically everything about Chinese culture—modes of dress and deportment, the value of age, hierarchy, and tradition, the nature of learning, knowledge, and language, the order and meaning of social relationships, and the value of the individual. Some of their most passionate critiques attacked the family and the tradition of arranged marriages. New Culture radicals insisted on the individual's right to happiness and self-determination and they promoted these values as a means to both individual fulfillment and state-strengthening. They argued that happy individuals were productive and that productive individuals were what China needed in order to regain its place in the world. To this end, they decried the traditional practice whereby families arranged their children's marriages and chose spouses who best met the families' needs. They insisted on the importance of marrying for love and so demanded the right to choose their own wives and husbands. They argued that the traditional *da jiazu* (joint family) be replaced by the *xiao jiating* (literally "small family"), a term which is best translated as "conjugal family." The *xiao jiating* made the couple the center of the family and emphasized the emotional attachment and life interests that bound husband and wife together. In addition to emotional independence from the joint family, the *xiao jiating* ideal prescribed economic and spatial independence too. Husbands and wives would support themselves and live by themselves with their children.

The legal precedents to the PRC's marriage law can also be traced to about this time. The Beijing Supreme Court saw itself as a leading force in social reform and beginning in 1916 it steadily reduced the family's prerogative in governing the marital life of its children. In 1927, the Nationalists' Supreme Court continued this reformist tradition. In the spring of 1931 the Nationalist government promulgated its Family Law. In principle, and often in detail, the Nationalists' and the Communists' marriage codes were strikingly similar. Like the codes supported by the Communists in their various soviets before 1949, and like the New Marriage Law of 1950, the Nationalists' code of 1931 guaranteed the individual's right to choose his or her spouse. It also provided equal divorce rights for men and women. In fact, most of what the Communist Party touted as its own innovation can be found in the Nationalists' family law. The similarities in the codes arose in part because the two parties drew on a similar pool of recruits in the early and mid 1920s (i.e. former New Culture radicals) and in part because the two parties shared remarkably congruent state-building goals.

In the mid to late 1920s, the family ideals championed by New Culture radicals spread rapidly into progressive urban circles. By the early 1930s, these ideas had won acceptance among petty urbanites, progressive entrepreneurs, and the social elite of China's modernizing cities — especially those of Shanghai. (Shanghai dominated Republican print culture and it was largely through the periodicals and books that poured out of Shanghai that intellectual trends of the Republican period were shared among China's large cities.) The popularity of the ideals of romantic love and marriage are attested to by the efforts that the CCP made to remold these ideas to fit a revolutionary program once the Party came to power in 1949.

When the PRC promulgated its New Marriage Law in 1950, the ideas it embodied had been familiar to many of China's urbanites for thirty years. These precedents were so rich and influential that the PRC's efforts can best be described as a culmination of the ideas, legislation, and practices of the previous three and a half decades. Although the Communist Party was not, in fact, the sole advocate of women's rights and marriage reform, the Communists' contributions were significant: the PRC's codification of marriage law was coupled with the potential for enforcement that far exceeded the ability of any previous governing or political body and, unlike urban proponents of family reform in the Republican period, the Communists succeeded in carrying reform into the countryside.

LI FENGJIN   (Prologue)

This true story is very moving. It is a typical representation of feudal marriage in rural Jiangnan.¹ And it communicates the feeling of the struggle between the old and the new.

On the one hand we remember how women in the old society suffered the cruelty and coercion of feudalism and on the other hand we want to use this story to carry the new democratic marriage law to the masses. It is a lively teaching tool.

Lastly, we want to congratulate Li Fengjin for achieving liberation under the protection of the New Marriage Law of the People's Government. And, moreover, to congratulate the women of all of China who, under the leadership of Chairman Mao and the People's Government have broken out of the feudal shackles that have held them for several thousand years and for achieving liberation.

Let this little volume serve as a souvenir of today's promulgation of the New Marriage Law!

Li Fengjin[2] was the daughter of a poor family in Sanyuan village in New Maple township in the district of Maple Bridge in Suzhou.

When she was eight years old, her mother received twenty dan[3] of rice from Tang Jinrong[4] in a neighboring village as a betrothal gift marking her marriage engagement to him.

If I don't go, do you mean to say you would let us starve to death?

You won't listen to me. If the Tang's find out you have gone to work as a servant and oppose it, there is nothing I can do.

When Li Fengjin was fifteen years old, she went to the city to work in order to support her mother.

Li Fengjin worked in the city as a servant for six years. When she was twenty-one she completed the commercial transaction that was her marriage to Tang Jinrong.[5]

She could not stand the Tang family's abuse. The only thing for her to do was to flee back to her mother's house.

Her mother could not support her and sent her back.[7]

When she returned to the Tang home the brothers would not even give her food to eat. She secretly ate pig food and so was beaten time and time again.

She wanted to separate from Tang Jinrong but her feudal-minded mother absolutely refused.

Daughters of good families cannot just divorce whenever they please. Moreover, they gave twenty dan of rice as a betrothal gift. Tell me, how could I face them?

In Sanyuan village there was a young farm hand named Gu Shuijin.[8] He was very angry about this circumstance.

It is a pity, Li Fengjin was beaten by her husband again.

A woman beaten and wounded by a barbarous husband, We ought to help her!

And so, Gu Shuijin often went to Li Fengjin's house to ask after her.

Gu Shuijin sympathized with her. He encouraged her to rebel. Gradually they became close friends.

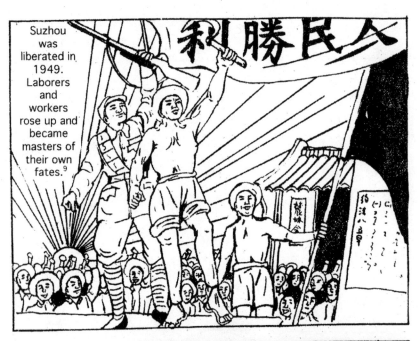

Suzhou was liberated in 1949. Laborers and workers rose up and became masters of their own fates.[9]

In 1950, the Central People's Government promulgated the New Marriage Law. When Li Fengjin learned of it, she was extremely happy.[10]

The feudal-minded people of their village embellished the facts of Li Fengjin and Gu Shuijin's relationship and passed the story about so that the whole village knew it.

If her husband finds out he'll beat her half to death again.

Fengjin and Gu Shuijin are a little untrustworthy.

Li Fengjin had her fill of suffering from her neighbors' ridicule. She could not stay at her mother's house and had no alternative but to return to her husband's home.[11]

On the day of the mediation, Jin township chief did not support Li Fengjin. On the contrary, he told her to go back to Tang Jinrong.

Although Li Fengjin was not willing, she was forced back into "prostitution."

It's better that you just go ahead and kill me than treat me like this.

Li Fengjin returned to the Tang home. It was a living hell.

Li Fengjin jumped over the wall and fled.

Before long they're going to beat me to death. Help me think of something.

I will certainly help you think of a way.

She didn't dare return to her mother's home so she went to Gu Shuijin's to beg for help.

Tang Jinrong won't find you living here. You should stop worrying.

You saved me from prostitution. Now I can live happily!

Gu Shuijin found a house next to Hengtang River. The two lived together.[14]

After Tang Jinrong found out where they lived, he called on his family and friends to gather at his house and discuss what to do.

So Tang Jinrong led friends and family to the Hengtang River to look for them.

Their barbarous feudal behavior was discovered by the cadres of a work unit that was passing by.

My wife had an affair. Our village has always punished people this way.

In the liberated areas this kind of reckless disorder is not allowed.

The cadres of the work unit immediately came and stopped this abuse and untied Fengjin and Shuijin.

The work unit cadres took them all to the seat of the township government in order to take care of the matter.[15]

Fengjin and I are living together because we both want to.

I was married to Tang Jinrong in a feudal marriage. He has abused me many times. I am living with Shuijin completely of my own accord. It is acceptable according to the law.

Gu Shuijin seduced a married woman and Li Fengjin took a lover and ran off. Both should be punished.

Township chief Jin had not left behind the old officious ways. He very sternly interrogated Fengjin and Shuijin.

22

A battalion chief of the People's Army, Zhou Xiaodi, helped township chief Jin put Gu Shuijin in the pig pen and he even administered corporal punishment.

Li Fengjin was again handed over to Tang Jinrong to take back home.

Gu Shuijin's father went to the township government asking that his son be released to him on bail, but the township chief refused.

My son has severe injuries. I'm begging you to let him come home so we can take care of him.

Your son has committed a crime and cannot be released.

Tang Jinrong and his brother put Li Fengjin in chains in the grinding room.

24

Li Fengjin went hungry for two nights. Tang Jinrong beat her cruelly with a wooden club. Moreover, he wanted her to grind grain.

楓橋區人民政府

Township Chief Jin only listened to the Tangs' side of the story. He put Shuijin in a pig pen. Fengjin was locked in the Tang family's grinding room. I beg the District Chief to act strictly according to official rules.

Township Chief Jin's style is wrong. I will send people right now to go release them.

Gu Shuijin's father went to the Maple Bridge District People's Government[16] to complain. He begged them to release Shuijin and Fengjin.

You two go on back. If anyone comes to bully you again, come to the district government and report it.[17]

The Maple Bridge District Chief sent a cadre to the county government who released Li Fengjin and Gu Shuijin and let them go back home.

When the people of Maple Bridge District heard about this they were extremely dissatisfied, so they wrote a letter to the New Suzhou News asking the government to look into it further.[18]

On June 1, the New Suzhou News published this letter. Everyone in the city paid it serious attention.[19]

The Sunan Judicial Department and the Suzhou District People's Civil Court also learned about this affair. They consulted with the Wu County Judicial Section of the People's Government.

After consultation they formed a small investigative group that went to New Maple Township to do first hand investigation. As a result of the investigation they discovered the truth.

The Wu County Judicial Section of the People's Government questioned those involved in the case and resolved it rationally.

Wu County Judicial Section called a meeting of cadres and the masses at Majiabing, a village of New Maple Township.

Today, in order to fully execute the spirit of the New Marriage Law, we have called a cadres-and-masses meeting. Please each express his or her opinion.[20]

I was unwilling to study the New Marriage Law. I used a very subjective point of view to handle the matter. That was wrong. Only after study did I finally understand the bondage women previously suffered under feudalism. Under the policies of the new democratic government, we must smash feudalism. Men and women are equal and they should enthusiastically unite and produce in order to construct a new China. [21]

Jin Township Chief also criticized his own actions. Those who were unclear about the New Marriage Law received a good lesson.

29

Li Fengjin and Tang Jinrong are given permission to dissolve their marital relationship. Li Fengjin's personal property should all go to her. [22]

On the spot they publicly announced the marriage case of Li Fengjin and Tang Jinrong.

The suit against Tang Jinrong and Tang Gouda for harming Li Fengjin and beating Gu Shuijin was also decided at the same time. It was decided that they should be punished.

It was also appropriate to punish Township Chief Jin and Zhou Xiaodi. All the masses gathered there supported this rational verdict.

This meeting allowed the New Marriage Law to really penetrate the countryside. Every person achieved an accurate understanding.

The people of New Maple District no longer looked down upon Li Fengjin and Gu Shuijin. Rather, they understood that they were legally husband and wife.

Li Fengjin and Gu Shuijin were free, happy, and hard working.

We should return the government's benevolence with enthusiastic production and support for the front line.

We are grateful to the Communist Party and to Chairman Mao.[23]

The People's Government of Wu County called a meeting of the masses. They presented the marriage case of Li Fengjin as an example through which to further educate the masses about the marriage law.

Today we want to advance the masses' education about the New Marriage Law. We have especially made Li Fengjin's marriage case the center of discussion. She will open the meeting.[24]

I am a woman who experienced the compulsion and harm of a feudal marriage. My days were filled with suffering. Since I received the protection of the Central Government's New Marriage Law, I have begun, with all the rest of my Chinese sisters, to stand up.

And Li Fengjin spoke.

The feudal society of the past buried the lives and happiness of unknown numbers of women.[25]

Under the protection of the new democratic New Marriage Law, the women of today's China have smashed their feudal shackles and achieved freedom, equality, and happiness.[26]

Notes

1. Jiangnan, i.e. that part of Jiangsu province south of the Yangzi River.

2. Literally, "phoenix gold."

3. *Dan* is a dry measure for grain that equals 120-160 pounds. It is roughly equivalent to the picul.

4. His given name, Jinrong, literally means "flourishing gold," i.e. to become rich. It also rhymes with the *jinrong* meaning finance. The editors are making a not-too-subtle reference to a common characterization of the traditional marriage system as a market in which women were bought and sold. Note also that in the bottom frame of page 14, Li Fengjin is forcibly returned to her husband. The narrative comments that she was "forced back into 'prostitution.'" Critics of the traditional marriage system often equated arranged marriage to prostitution, arguing that in marriage the husband's family was really simply purchasing the woman's reproductive and sexual services.

5. The structure in the foreground is a memorial arch to a chaste widow—someone who had been widowed early in marriage, usually while in her late teens, and who had remained unmarried and celibate into menopause (and presumably until her death). In the background we see a procession in which a bride is being carried to her husband's house by a sedan chair. Both of these images signal to the reader the defining characteristics of the traditional arranged marriage: it was arranged by families with family, rather than individual, interests in mind; the bride and groom usually had never seen one another; women generally went to live with their husband's family; wives were expected to be virgins before marriage and forever chaste after. The skulls in the grass are a blunt reminder of all the women's lives lost to "feudalism."

6. Literally, "Dog big." To use the word "dog" in a Chinese epithet has much the same derisive connotation that it does in American English. Notice the fedora, a hat that denoted the villain in much Republican era (1912-1949) fiction and film. The brothers' long gowns tell us that they do not make their living through manual labor.

7. Notice that her mother sends her back only because she is too poor to feed her.

8. Literally, "Water gold."

9. The banner overhead says, "The People are victorious."

10. Note that Gu Shuijin is reading it to her. Like most rural women, Li Fengjin was probably illiterate.

11. Note that Li Fengjin's mother objects to her leaving Tang, but still allows her daughter to stay in her natal home. In fact, despite traditional claims that daughters were like "spilt water," in fact, women often relied on natal families for help and refuge when life at their husbands' homes became difficult. See, for example, Mann, Judd, and Theiss.

35

12. The character in the upper right corner is *fu*, meaning happiness and good fortune. Paper squares printed with this character were typically pasted upside down on windows and walls to welcome the lunar New Year. The character was placed upside down because the word for arrive, *dao*, sounds like the word for upside down. Thus "fu" upside down is a pun for "fu" arrives. Here, however, the character is right side up, signalling that happiness and good fortune have not visited the Tang household.

13. Sounds like "Increase money."

14. Confucian morality to the contrary, it seems that premarital and extramarital sex, as well as cohabitation without the sanction of marriage, was not that unusual in the countryside. See, for example, Mao, Sommer, and Theiss.

15. The wall slogan says "Help yourselves through production."

16. The placard says "The People's Government of Maple Bridge District."

17. Note that widows' chastity arches stand before them as they turn toward home, signifying that they are reentering feudal territory.

18. During the Republican era, letters to the editor had become an important format for the exchange and the molding of public opinion. See Yeh.

19. The placard displays the name of a Daoist temple—Temple of the Abstruse. The newspaper office is probably located in the small, ramshackle building to the right of the temple gate. It is interesting that government propaganda included the depiction of a religious building. The illustrator may have intended to contrast the looming superstition of the old order with the truth offered in the modern, government-run, press—note the paperboy in the foreground of the frame offering a paper for sale.

20. Public trials were a common CCP technique for indoctrinating the population on Party laws, rules, and interpretation. Probably the most famous are the many such "trials" of the Cultural Revolution, but they were used at other times too. See Diamant for some discussion of public trials that were used to introduce the New Marriage Law.

21. Which is exactly what we will see our hero and heroine doing on page 32.

22. That is to say, none of it was to be used to reimburse the Tangs.

23. The sun in the background can, and probably was, read as a reference to Mao.

24. Note that Chairman Mao presides over the trial in absentia via the portrait that is hung above the podium.

25. Observe that the chaste widow arch in the foreground is falling apart.

26. The banners read (from top to bottom): "Women have stood up," "Destroy the feudal system," "Protect the New Marriage Law," "Long live Chairman Mao."

Appendix

The 1950 Marriage Law

General Principles
Article 1. The feudal marriage system based on arbitrary and compulsory arrangements and the supremacy of man over woman, and in disregard of the interests of the children, is abolished.

The new democratic marriage system, which is based on the free choice of partners, on monogamy, on equal rights for both sexes, and on the protection of the lawful interests of women and children, is put into effect.

Article 2. Bigamy, concubinage, child betrothal, interference in the remarriage of widows, and the exaction of money or gifts in connection with marriages, are prohibited.

The Marriage Contract
Article 3. Marriage is based upon the complete willingness of the two parties. Neither party shall use compulsion and no third party is allowed to interfere.

Article 4. A marriage can be contracted only after the man has reached twenty years of age and the women eighteen years of age.

Article 5. No man or woman is allowed to marry in any of the following instances:

(a) Where the man and woman are lineal relatives by blood or where the man and woman are brother and sister born of the same parents or where the man and the women are half brother and half sister. The question of prohibiting marriage between collateral relatives by blood (up to the fifth degree of relationship) is determined by custom.

(b) Where one party, because of certain physical defects, is sexually impotent.

(c) Where one party is suffering from venereal disease, mental disorder, leprosy, or any other disease which is regarded by medical science as rendering a person unfit for marriage.

Article 6. In order to contract a marriage, both the man and the woman should register in person with the people's government of the district or township in which they reside. If the proposed marriage is found to be in conformity with the provisions of the law, the local people's government should, without delay, issue marriage certificates.

If the proposed marriage is not found to be in conformity with the provisions of this law, registration should not be granted.

Rights and Duties of Husband and Wife
Article 7. Husband and wife are companions living together and enjoy equal status in the home.

Article 8. Husband and wife are in duty bound to love, respect, assist, and look after each other, to live in harmony, to engage in productive work, to care for their children, and to strive jointly for the welfare of the family and for the building up of the new society.

Article 9. Both husband and wife have the right to free choice of occupation and free participation in work or in social activities.

Article 10. Husband and wife have equal rights in the possession and management of family property.

Article 11. Husband and wife have the right to use his or her own family name.

Article 12. Husband and wife have the right to inherit each other's property.

Relations between Parents and Children

Article 13. Parents have the duty to rear and to educate their children; the children have the duty to support and to assist their parents. Neither the parents nor the children shall maltreat or desert one another.

The foregoing provision also applies to foster parents and foster children.

Infanticide by drowning and similar criminal acts are strictly prohibited.

Article 14. Parents and children have the right to inherit one another's property.

Article 15. Children born out of wedlock enjoy the same rights as children born in lawful wedlock. No person is allowed to harm them or discriminate against them.

Where the paternity of a child born out of wedlock is legally established by the mother of the child or by other witnesses or material evidence, the identified father must bear the whole of part of the cost of maintenance and education of the child until the age of eighteen.

With the consent of the mother, the natural father may have custody of the child.

With regard to the maintenance of a child born out of wedlock, if its mother marries, the provisions of Article 22 apply.

Article 16. Neither husband nor wife may maltreat or discriminate against children born of a previous marriage by either party and in that party's custody.

Divorce

Article 17. Divorce is granted when husband and wife both desire it. In the event the husband or the wife alone insist upon divorce, it may be granted only when mediation by the district people's government and the judicial organ has failed to bring about a reconciliation.

In cases where divorce is desired by both husband and wife, both parties should register with the district people's government in order to obtain divorce certificates. The district people's government, after establishing that divorce is desired by both parties and that appropriate measures have been taken for the care of children and property, should issue the divorce certificates without delay.

When one party insists on divorce, the district people's government may try to effect a reconciliation. If such mediation fails, it should, without delay, refer the case to the county or municipal people's court for decision. The district people's government should not attempt to prevent or to obstruct either party from appealing to the county or municipal people's court. In dealing with a divorce case, the county or municipal people's court should, in the first instance, try to bring about a reconciliation between the parties. In case such mediation fails, the court should render a decision without delay.

After divorce, if both husband and wife desire the resumption of marriage relations, they should apply to the district people's government for a registration of remarriage. The district people's government should accept such a registration and issue certificates of remarriage.

Article 18. The husband is not allowed to apply for a divorce when his wife is pregnant, and may apply for divorce only one year after the birth of the child. In the case of a woman applying for divorce, this restriction does not apply.

Article 19. In the case of a member of the revolutionary army on active service who maintains correspondence with his or her family, that army member's consent must be obtained before his or her spouse may apply for divorce.

Divorce may be granted to the spouse of a member of the revolutionary army who does not correspond with his or her family for a period of two years subsequent to the date of the promulgation of this law. Divorce may also be granted to the spouse of a member of the revolutionary army, who had not maintained correspondence with his or her family for over two years prior to the promulgation of this law, and who fails to correspond with his of her family for a further period of one year subsequent to the promulgation of the present law.

Maintenance and Education of Children after Divorce

Article 20. The blood ties between parents and children are not ended by the divorce of the parents. No matter whether the father or the mother has the custody of the children, they remain the children of both parties.

After divorce, both parents continue to have the duty to support and educate their children.

After divorce, the guiding principle is to allow the mother to have the custody of a breast-fed infant. After the weaning of the child, if a dispute arises between the two parties over the guardianship and an agreement cannot be reached, the people's court should render a decision in accordance with the interest of the child.

Article 21. If, after divorce, the mother is given custody of a child, the father is responsible for the whole or part of the necessary cost of the maintenance and education of the child. Both parties should reach an agreement regarding the amount and the duration of such maintenance and education. Lacking such an agreement, the people's court should render a decision.

Payment may be made in cash, in kind, or by tilling land allocated to the child.

An agreement reached between parents or a decision rendered by the people's court in connect with the maintenance and education of the child does not obstruct the child from requesting either parent to increase the amount decided upon by agreement or by judicial decision.

Article 22. In the case where a divorced woman remarries and her husband is willing to pay the whole or part of the cost of maintaining and educating the child or children by her former husband, the father of the child or children is entitled to have such cost of maintenance and education reduced or to be exempted from bearing such cost in accordance with the circumstances.

Property and Maintenance after Divorce

Article 23. In case of divorce, the wife retains such property as belonged to her prior to her marriage. The disposal of other family property is subject to agreement between the two parties. In cases where agreement cannot be reached, the people's court should render a decision after taking into consideration the actual state of the family property, the interests of the wife and the child or children, and the principles of benefiting the development of production.

In cases in which the property allocated to the wife and her child or children is sufficient for the maintenance and education of the child or children, the husband may be exempted from bearing further maintenance and education costs.

Article 24. In case of divorce, debts incurred jointly by husband and wife during the period of their married life should be paid out of the property jointly acquired by them during this period. In cases where no such property has been acquired or in cases where such property is insufficient to pay off such debts, the husband is held responsible for paying them. Debts incurred separately by the husband or wife should be paid off by the party responsible.

Article 25. After divorce, if one party has not remarried and has maintenance difficulties, the other party should render assistance. Both parties should work out an agreement with regard to the method and duration of such assistance; in case an agreement cannot be reached, the people's court should render a decision.

By-Laws

Article 26. Persons violating this law will be punished in accordance with law. In cases where interference with the freedom of marriage had caused death or injury to one or both parties, persons guilty of such interference will bear responsibility for the crime before the law.

Article 27. This law comes into force from the date of its promulgation. In regions inhabited by minority nationalities in compact communities, the People's Government (or the military and administrative committee) of the greater administrative area or the Provincial People's Government may enact certain modifications or supplementary articles in conformity with the actual conditions prevailing among minority nationalities in regard to marriage. But such measures must be submitted to the government administration council for ratification before enforcement.

Selected Bibliography of English Language Sources

Andors, Phyllis. *The Unfinished Liberation of Chinese Women, 1949-1980*. Blooming-
ton: Indiana University Press, 1983.

Barlow, Tani. "Theorizing Woman: Funü, Guojia, Jiating [Chinese Women, Chinese
State, Chinese Family]." *Genders* , no. 10 (March 1991): 132-160.

Beahan, Charlotte L. "Feminism and Nationalism in the Chinese Women's Press, 1902-
1911." *Modern China* 1, no. 4 (October 1975): 379-415.

Bernhardt, Kathryn, and Philip C. C. Huang, eds. *Civil Law in Qing and Republican
China*. Stanford: Stanford University Press, 1994.

Brownell, Susan and Jeffrey Wasserstrom, eds. Chinese *Femininities/Chinese Mascu-
linities*. Berkeley: University of California Press, 2002.

Buxbaum, David, ed. Chinese *Family Law and Social Change*. Seattle: University of
Washington Press, 1978.

Chow, Tse-tsung. *The May Fourth Movement: Intellectual Revolution in Modern China*.
Cambridge: Harvard University Press, 1960.

Croll, Elizabeth. *Feminism and Socialism in China*. Boston: Routledge & Kegan Paul,
1978.

Diamant, Neil. *Revolutionizing the Family: Politics, Love, and Divorce in Urban and
Rural China, 1949-1968*. Berkeley: University of California Press, 2000.

Gilmartin, Christina. *Engendering the Chinese Revolution: Radical Women, Communist Politics, and Mass Movement in the 1920s*. Berkeley: University of California
Press, 1995.

Glosser, Susan. *Chinese Visions of Family and State, 1915-1953*. Berkeley: University of
California Press, 2003.

Hsia, Ching-lin et. al, trans. *The Civil Code of the Republic of China, Book IV and Book
V*. Shanghai: Kelly & Walsh Limited, 1931.

Hu, Chi-hsi. "The Sexual Revolution in the Kiangsi Soviet." *The China Quarterly* 59
(July 1974): 477-490.

Johnson, Kay Ann. *Women, the Family, and Peasant Revolution in China*. Chicago:
University of Chicago Press, 1983.

Judd, Ellen. "Niangjia: Chinese Women and Their Natal Families." *The Journal of Asian
Studies* 48, no. 3 (August 1989): 525-544.

Lang, Olga. *Chinese Family and Society*. New Haven, CT: Yale University Press, 1946.

Mann, Susan. "The Cult of Domesticity in Republican Shanghai's Middle Class." *Jindai
Zhongguo funü shi yanjiu* (Research of Women in Modern Chinese History) 2
(June 1994).

---. "Grooming a Daughter for Marriage: Brides and Wives in the Mid-Ch'ing Period."
In *Marriage and Inequality in Chinese Society*, eds. Rubie Watson and Patricia
Ebrey. Berkeley: University of California Press, 1995.

McDermott, Joseph P. "The Domestic Bursar." *Tradition and Modernization: Essays in
Honour of the Seventieth Birthday of Professor Kiyoko Takeda Cho*, ed. Uozumi
Masayoshi. Tokyo: International Christian University, 1990.

Meijer, M. J. *Marriage Law and Policy in the Chinese People's Republic*. Hong Kong: Hong Kong University Press, 1971.

Ono, Kazuko. *Chinese Women in a Century of Revolution, 1850-1950*, trans. Joshua Fogel. Stanford: Stanford University Press, 1989.

Pa, Chin. *Family*. New York: Anchor Books, 1972.

Roy, Tod, trans. *The Plum in the Golden Vase or Chin P'ing Mei*. (Vol. 1: The Gathering) Princeton: Princeton University Press, 1993.

Schwarcz, Vera. "Ibsen's Nora: The Promise and the Trap." *Bulletin for Concerned Asian Scholars* 7, no. 1 (January 1975):

Schwartz, Benjamin. *In Search of Wealth and Power: Yen Fu and the West*. Cambridge, MA: Belknap Press, 1983.

Sommer, Mathew. *Sex, Law and Society in Late Imperial China*. Stanford: University of Stanford Press, 2000.

Stacey, Judith. *Patriarchy and Socialist Revolution in China*. Berkeley: University of California Press, 1983.

Stranahan, Patricia. *Yan'an Women and the Communist Party*. Berkeley: Institute of East Asian Studies, University of California, 1983.

Theiss, Janet. *Disgraceful Matters: The Politics of Chastity in Eighteenth-Century China*. Berkeley: University of California Press, 2004.

Valk, Marius Hendrikus van der. *Conservatism in Modern Chinese Family Law*. Leiden, Netherlands: E. J. Brill, 1956.

---. *Interpretations of the Supreme Court at Peking*. Batavia: Indonesia, 1949.

---. "Freedom of Marriage in Modern Chinese Law." Monumenta Serica 3 (1938): 1-34.

Wang, Zheng. *Women in the Chinese Enlightenment: Oral and Textual Histories*. Berkeley: University of California Press, 1999.

Witke, Roxane. "Mao Tse-tung, Women and Suicide." *China Quarterly*, no. 31 (July 1967): 128-147.

---. "Transformation of Attitudes towards Women during the May Fourth Era of Modern China." Ph.D. diss., University of California, 1970.

Wolf, Margery. *Revolution Postponed: Women in Contemporary China*. Stanford: Stanford University Press, 1989.

Yeh, Wen-hsin. "Progressive Journalism and Shanghai's Petty Urbanites: Zou Taofen and the Shenghuo Enterprise, 1926-1945." In *Shanghai Sojourners*, eds. Wen-hsin Yeh and Frederic Wakeman, Jr. Berkeley: Institute of East Asian Studies, University of California, 1992.